Presented to:

_____

From:

_____

Date:

_____

A
Generous
Life

A Generous Life

10 Steps to Living a Life Money Can't Buy

DAVID GREEN
with BILL HIGH

ZONDERVAN®

This book is dedicated to those seeking to live out the generous and joyful life. May you find your inspiration in Jesus, the author and perfecter of the ultimately generous life. He gave it all.

Contents

CONTENTS

Introduction

write with the benefit of hindsight. Some might call it a rearview mirror. I'm nearly seventy-seven years old, and when I was younger, I never could have imagined how my life would turn out.

I never dreamed that my little business, started inside of my garage in 1972, would one day employ thirty-five thousand employees and process billions of dollars in annual sales. Nor did I dream that our business would one day be able to give away 50 percent of its profits, providing fuel for the gospel around the world. That picture of reaching the nations would have brought tears to my parents' eyes.

Over the course of my life, I've made newspaper headlines, written books, appeared on television and radio shows, and spoken to large audiences. No one would have picked me for any of those assignments in my growing-up years. And certainly no one—particularly me—would have ever dreamed I'd sit in the United States Supreme Court, listening to lawyers argue my case.

I've lived a truly wonderful life. But the blessings I've experienced do not rest in the possessions or accomplishments I've accumulated. Instead, my greatest blessings are those things that cannot be measured. I heard it said once, "Not all things that count can be counted." I'd like to share with you some of my lessons for living the kind of life that money cannot buy.

I was raised in the Southwest, down red dirt roads lined by cotton fields. I grew up in small towns where drivers waved to every passerby, where store clerks knew their customers by first name. In every town where we lived, I was known as the preacher's son, the fifth of six children from Walter and Marie

Green. Everything that I have and all that I long to pass on to my descendants has grown from the riches Walter and Marie Green embedded in my life.

Do you remember doilies? They were crocheted mats that people might use for decoration on a table or a sofa. On top of taking care of a big family and a big garden, and being a pastor's wife, my mother used to crochet doilies and sell them. Why? Even though my parents gave money together for missions, my mother wanted to make her own offering for missions. So she sold doilies. That memory still sticks with me.

My parents' legacy consisted of hard work, sacrifice, and an eye on eternity. In this sense alone, I can say that I was born into a wealthy family.

As surprising as it may sound, my parents were also some of the most generous people I've ever known. Their spare living and meager income did not stop them from being generous in a thousand different ways. Mother may have had only three or four dresses in her closet, but if she heard of a woman who needed one, you could be sure Mother would soon arrive at the woman's doorstep with a dress in hand. Such acts were repeated time and again.

The most stunning evidence I ever saw of my parents' generosity came late in the 1960s. My younger brother, James, offered to help my father put his financial books in order. Working through records from many years, James concluded that the most my father ever made in a week was a paltry $138.

We weren't that surprised when we heard this. We always knew our parents received little money in return for their labors. What astonished us, though, were the many canceled checks written to churches for as much as $100. We soon realized that our parents often gave almost their entire weekly salary back to the churches they served. What amazing generosity! What big souls!

More than anyone else, my mother taught me the difference between what is temporal and what is eternal. James 4:14 says, "What is your life? You are a mist that appears for a little while and then vanishes."

A legacy of true value is a legacy made of more than money. A true legacy remembers the brevity of life. It is conceived in wisdom, nurtured by principle, and sustained by character. If we pass only money to the next generation, we lay a crushing load upon them. The inheritance of greater value is the sum of how we live, what we believe, and the content of the dreams that carry us to success. This is what the next generation needs most from us, and what that next generation must prepare to hand off as well.

To hand off this kind of legacy, we must first live it out in our own lives. In the pages ahead, I propose a different way of living life, a way that I have learned through trial and error over my lifetime. This way is a foolproof road that has stood the test of time for generations. It has brought joy, peace, and contentment for thousands of years, but it's a road that is being forgotten today. In today's world, it seems that the goal is to make money, and then make more money, until we can finally buy everything we want. Unfortunately, what we really want can't be bought.

We want love.

We want happiness.

We want peace.

We want security.

In essence, we want a life that money can't buy, yet we're chasing money to get there. There is a different way to live. As you read, I will lay out ten steps that I have found revolutionary in my own life. These ten steps are basic concepts, some of which you may have heard before, such as giving generously, seeing yourself as a steward, and living for eternity. The key, however, is in making and implementing a plan. The steps don't work as ideas; they work as action. Throughout this book, you'll read about times when I wrote down my goals and discussed them with family members. I've found that real transformation happens when you write down a plan and talk

> A true legacy . . . is conceived in wisdom, nurtured by principle, and sustained by character.

about it with a friend or family member. If you live out the ten steps, they will transform your life and give you a life that money cannot buy.

STEP 1

Make the End
the Beginning

The questions we ask at the end of life
are the ones we should begin with.

A fellow CEO told me his story slowly and sadly. He'd stepped into business full of youthful energy. He was out to prove to his father that he was "something" after all. So he threw himself into growing a business. Long days overflowed into evenings. Those days often included Saturdays—maybe Sundays too. But it was a price he was willing to pay.

To his credit, the business grew. Locations were added. More employees. More sales. More hours. More stress. Somewhere in the background, his wife and children were there amid all his activity. He didn't realize the toll his work was taking on him and his family. He knew his wife prayed for him, and he appreciated that. He thought it was nice to have God on his side too.

He came to a conference where I was speaking. He admitted that he didn't really know what life was all about, but for the first time he heard from other men about a different measuring stick—something more than sales. He heard about a life of generosity—of giving to help others. And he wondered if there was something more. Perhaps the ladder he was climbing leaned against the wrong wall.

The questions are different at different stages of life.

In our twenties we tend to ask, "Who will I marry?" and "What will my career be?" In our thirties we may ask, "How can I advance in my career?" and "How will my kids turn out?"

By the forties we start to ask, "Is this the job I really

wanted?" and "Why is life so hard?" In our fifties we start to look both backward and forward: "How has it turned out so far?" and "What will I do that's significant in the next twenty-five years?"

By our sixties, we ask simpler questions, like, "Will my health hold out?" and "When will I see my grandchildren?" By our seventies and eighties, we really start to look back and ask, "Was it all worth it?" or "Will anyone remember?" We might even ask, "Should I have, could I have, given more?"

The funny thing about the questions of life is that the ones we ask at the end are the ones we should begin with. It is tough to craft a meaningful life without considering our end: What do we hope for, what do we dream for, relative to our lives, our family, our children?

In particular, I hope that some of the questions that we put off—about our mortality, about our sense of meaning and success—we can begin to address right now. And that we'll find we are talking not about endings but about enduring legacies.

What is a legacy, anyway?

The dictionary gives two definitions. First, a legacy is an amount of money or property passed to someone in a will. Second, a legacy is a thing handed down by a predecessor. I want to use the second definition because I believe it includes everything—from belief to right action to finances. You and I possess so much to hand down to our descendants, things seen and unseen.

Everyone has a legacy. Legacies cannot be neutral. Each person leaves either a good legacy or a bad legacy. Thankfully, we get to choose which kind of legacy we leave.

Fierce Faith

It has often brought a smile to my face to think that if Hobby Lobby had existed during the years I was growing up, my mother might never have darkened the door of one of our stores. Her attention was fixed on beautiful things of another kind, like our family, and her spending was limited by the challenging life she and my father chose to live.

My childhood was shaped by my father's work as a pastor in rural churches across Arizona, New Mexico, Texas, and Oklahoma. In a practice that was common among religious denominations at that time, Dad was assigned to a new church about every two years. For me, this meant eight different schools by the time I finished high school. None of these churches ever seemed to grow much larger than a hundred souls. As a result, small towns, small churches, and small incomes defined our lives, making it a constant challenge for my parents to care for our family of eight.

> The funny thing about the questions of life is that the ones we ask at the end are the ones we should begin with.

What I learned from the fierce faith of my parents has shaped every day of my life since. They may not have been rich by the world's standards, but their influence on my life is inestimable. Every decision they made was sifted through the question, "What will count for eternity?" I can still remember hearing their voices raised in prayer and how they cried out to God for their children and for the lost people of our various communities. The sound of their singing still plays in my mind and moves me deeply. Many times I would get up in the middle of the night and hear them praying or see them poring over God's Word, trying to center their life on biblical principles. They trusted in Jesus Christ completely, and because they did, we saw an almost unceasing stream of miracles. My faith grew as I saw God faithfully provide for our needs again and again.

I imagine my parents worried because I never did well in school. I had to repeat the seventh grade, and I barely got out of high school. I did love to read, but the classroom held almost no fascination for me, which is why I did so poorly.

One of the best things my teachers ever did for me was put me in a program of "distributive education." Today this would be called "work study." Whatever the name, the idea that I could get school credit for working a part-time job seemed like a miracle to me at the time. I landed at McClellan's, a five-and-dime store in Altus, Oklahoma. It was at this store I found my calling.

By the grace of God, I had success in the retail business from the start. My God-given gifts emerged, and I found new ways of doing things. Over the years I received promotions, earned pay increases, and enjoyed things my family had never been able to, like a car and a larger house. As this success came to me, my mother helped me keep things in an eternal perspective. I think she was proud of me, but she was also worried that I was becoming too entangled with the things of this world. Our conversations went something like this:

"Hey, Mom, I'm twenty-one, and the youngest store manager!"

"Yes, David, but what have you done for the Lord lately?"

"Hey, Mom, I'm now a district manager over all these stores."

"Yes, David, but what are you doing for the Lord?"

I could have become president of the United States and she would have said the same thing: "What are you doing for the Lord?" She understood that there was only one thing worth doing in this life, and that was serving God. Today I thank my father and mother for the perspective they instilled in their children. They taught us to start with the end in mind.

My parents viewed their existence through the lens of eternity. They remembered that at the end of their lives, the only endeavors that would count were the ones that lasted for eternity. While most people wait till the end of life to ask, "Was it all worth it?" my parents flipped this question around, asking at the early stages of life, "What will be worth it at the end of my life?" And they spent their time on that which would last beyond their lives. Instead of asking at the end of life, "Could I have given more?" they asked at the beginning, "How much can I give?" When it seemed they had given everything they could, they took the question a step further, asking, "Can I give even more?" Because they asked these questions at the beginning, when they reached the end of life, they had peace. They could look back on a life well lived.

My mother passed away in my sister's arms. At the time of my mother's passing, she sat up with vigor in her voice as she cried out, "Do you see them? Do you see them?"

"See what?" my sister asked.

"Angels."

My mother was not rich. She was the wife of a pastor of a small church. But in God's economy, she was vital because of the legacy she handed down to her children, grandchildren, and great-grandchildren. She lived her life with a heavenly mind-set. She kept the end goal as her starting point for every life decision. She didn't have worldly goods, but she had children who served God, grandchildren who served God, and many souls who came to Christ through her faithful service and giving.

And at the end of my mother's life, God himself sent a company of angels to welcome her into his kingdom. Many billionaires I know would have loved to trade places with her.

What will your ending be? When you are welcomed into heaven, will your endeavors from earth follow you there? Take some time to write down your answers to the following questions:

- *Will the things I'm living for be worth it one hundred years from now?*
- *Will I be glad I spent my life on them?*
- *Could I be giving more?*

You will never regret starting out with wisdom.

Recognize Everything Is God's

Generosity and legacy happen
only when we return everything
to the rightful owner.

When I was going to school, I played the clarinet. I'm not sure how that came to be my instrument of choice, but all I could do was squeak out some pitiful shrieks. It put me at the bottom of the food chain. I was last chair in the clarinet section.

Later, the director switched me to the tuba, and I found I could bellow out with the best of them. I'm not sure if it was because of that experience, but when my boys were growing up, my wife, Barbara, and I decided they should be piano players. They labored at it, and they complained a lot, until finally we let them quit.

Somewhere along the way, another relative of mine sat down at the piano. With little in the way of lessons, she played as if she were Mozart. Her talent was a gift from God. This story reminds me that everything we have is a gift from God. Whether our ability is playing an instrument or running a company, God is the One who bestows us with everything we have. It is his to give.

How do you and I get to the point where we can give everything away? Before we can give in such a way, we need to realize who owns everything in the first place. I always believed that everything I owned was God's, until reality tested me.

We had Christian advisors come and help Barbara and me with our trust and our estate. Essentially, they expected us to hand down our assets from one generation to the next. This is the normal thing to do, but I didn't feel comfortable with the idea. I knew if I set up my estate the way our advisors were recommending, I would be making my great-grandchildren millionaires before they were even born. I didn't feel good about that. Not that you can't inherit money and be okay. I knew my children and grandchildren were trustworthy. But I had seen too many statistics about handing down large sums of money to your children and grandchildren. Too many times, it just doesn't work. More and more, I see that wealth can be a hindrance if it's seen as something you own rather than steward.

> Wealth can be a hindrance if it's seen as something you own rather than steward.

One night I was praying about this out in the backyard. All of a sudden, right there under the Oklahoma night sky, something dramatic happened. I sensed God saying to me, *"This company belongs to me. Don't you touch it. It's mine."*

The force of these words jolted me. I connected them right away with the Bible story about the day King David and his people tried to move the ark of the covenant into Jerusalem using a cart. Everything went well until one of the handlers, a man named Uzzah, reached out to steady the ark as it went over a bump in the road. God struck him dead on the spot. Why? The Bible says it was "because of his irreverent act" (2 Samuel 6:7). The whole procession came to a grinding halt. Celebration turned into disaster.

> I sensed God saying to me, *"This company belongs to me. Don't you touch it. It's mine."*

I sensed immediately that my worry about Hobby Lobby was largely because there was too much human effort attempting to steady the ark of the company. I truly believed then, as I believe now, that Hobby Lobby is a company God allowed to be born and to endure. If we kept getting in his way, if we kept relying on human strengths and thinking, what kind of trouble awaited us?

I went back in the house and took out a piece of paper from my steno pad and wrote down, "I own Hobby Lobby. Signed, God."

From that moment on, it was crystal clear in my mind that this was not my corporation. I had always believed that in some general sense. I had always given God the glory for what Hobby Lobby had become. Yet now God's ownership of the company had come to me in searing revelation.

While I had always believed Hobby Lobby was blessed by God, after that night it was as though he had staked a personal claim. He was not just leaving it to me to acknowledge his ownership with my words. He was enforcing his ownership in my heart and throughout the company. It was as transforming for me that night as it became for our entire company over time.

Psalm 24:1 says, "The earth is the LORD's, and everything in it, the world, and all who live in it." After that night, I sensed that God was saying, "*If I own it, then you have nothing to give away.*"

That's why Barbara and I and our children decided to officially sign away all of our ownership in the company, even though it sits in our trust. Once God declared his ownership, the matter became very simple. I don't own Hobby Lobby. If I don't own it, I'm going to try to take care of it the way God would want. I'm not just going to go off and buy a yacht. I'm going to steward it the way God intended.

Since we knew we weren't owners, we wanted to sign paperwork officially saying what we already knew to be true. If God says it is his, we wanted to say it too. We signed a document stating that we couldn't touch the value of this company, but we would only get a paycheck. All of our family members—our children and grandchildren—work for a salary that is a fair wage for what they do. None of us have any ownership. To me, that's just scriptural.

The Rule of Peace

Our belief that Hobby Lobby belonged to God gave us peace in the years to come, especially when our company came face-to-face with the Supreme Court.

In 2012, the U.S. government passed a law requiring all businesses to provide insurance, including coverage for contraceptives, for their employees. Among the sixteen different contraceptives, there were four that we believed ended life after conception, which went against our conviction that human life is sacred and should not be ended lightly. I believe, as do millions of Americans, that once conception has taken place in a mother's body, a new human being exists. That life must be protected, cherished, and brought lovingly into the world. That child has rights from the moment it is conceived. So when the U.S. government ordered the company I had started and built on Christian principles to pay for the killing of human beings in the womb, I just couldn't do it. I had to file a lawsuit to stop this challenge to our values.

Our journey to the Supreme Court is a long story, which I share fully in the book *Giving It All Away . . . and Getting It All Back Again.*[1] But this journey tested our faith that God owns Hobby Lobby.

Since Hobby Lobby was God's, so was the decision to file a lawsuit. So was the future of the company. I told the media, "This company is not mine. It's God's, and I am going to lean on him, whether or not the company survives the outcome of the Supreme Court's decision on our case."

The case worked its way up through the court systems, starting locally with the U.S. District Court for the Western District of Oklahoma and eventually reaching the Supreme Court in a case called *Burwell v. Hobby Lobby Stores, Inc.* As I sat in that awe-inspiring courtroom in Washington, DC, with its soaring columns and regal furnishings, listening to the oral arguments of the case, I felt a deep, unshakable, undeniable peace.

I knew the company was on the line.

I knew huge matters of faith and justice would be decided in the coming months as a result of our case.

I also knew the world was watching.

In the midst of it all, I felt peace. My family and I knew who we were. We had a God-given mission. We also knew who the company belonged to. It belonged to God, and him alone. Based on this, we had designed some unusual plans for what would happen to the company after we were gone and how the wealth from it would be used. This is what gave me peace that day in the Supreme Court building.

I knew who I was.

I knew who my family was.

I knew who owned Hobby Lobby.

I knew why we were in that courtroom.

I knew who controlled my fate no matter what those justices decided. And peace reigned.

In June 2014, the court released the verdict of a 5–4 vote in favor of Hobby Lobby. It was a huge victory. I imagine that during the days preceding the court's ruling, we were the most prayed-for family in the world. It all paid off. God granted not just the Green family but also the cause of justice and righteousness a great victory. We were thankful beyond words.

Through the Supreme Court journey, I learned the wonderful riches of peace. And not just any peace, but the kind that passes all understanding (see Philippians 4:7). Generosity and legacy can happen only when we have the peace that recognizes everything is God's.

> I knew who controlled my fate no matter what those justices decided. And peace reigned.

Years before we ever decided to file a lawsuit, I had realized that Hobby Lobby belonged to God. That night as I prayed under the stars in my backyard, begging for the Lord to give us wisdom on how to pass down the company, he clearly showed me the company was his. That revelation has led to sustained peace over the years.

We can only have this supernatural peace when we recognize that God owns everything. This crazy kind of heavenly peace requires that you and I be willing to give up everything. No guarantees. No safety net. Getting it all back again is not part of the equation. Only the willingness to lay it all on the line. God already owns everything, so when we give up control of our belongings, we simply acknowledge what was true the whole time: it was his in the first place. We simply give it back to him.

Put People Before Profit

Choose the eternal in the everyday mundane.

About once every few months, I host a roundtable where I share with CEOs the business principles I've learned over the years. Sometimes, as I talk to these leaders of successful companies, I hear that they have achieved success at the cost of their marriages, their children, and even their faith. This grieves me.

I've had occasion to sit down with some of these executives individually. Here's what's interesting. No matter how strong their company or how large their sales, those accomplishments are never the key part of the conversation.

Inevitably, they want to talk about their marriages and their children. Sometimes I learn about trouble in a marriage or about addiction issues with a child. No matter how great their wealth, their first concern is their family. Our relationships are the great equalizer. Wealthy or not, we are all affected by them. Hobby Lobby could be ten times what it is today, but if I failed in my marriage, the business success would not be worth it.

We can pursue wealth, but our joy doesn't come from our wealth. It comes from our relationships—with the Lord, with our spouses, with our children, and with others. That joy comes from having virtue in how you treat them. Honoring the people in your life, respecting them, doing what's right, acting with integrity. This is true virtue, and it begins with people.

How you and I treat our spouses matters. How we treat

our children matters. How you and I treat our employees or coworkers matters. We can invest in our children, our close friends, and our relatives.

When I started out in life, I had a few modest plans. I can tell you exactly what they were. First, I wanted to be successful in business. Second, I wanted to have a great marriage. Third, I wanted to raise children who would serve God. And underlying all these was a greater goal, one that seemed so second nature that I didn't think to write it down. It was a given that the motivation for everything I did was to serve the Lord.

As my parents always said, only two things in life are eternal: God's Word and people's souls. As I set out to live my life, I put people first, before building profits and pursuing great achievements. People are

> Honoring the people in your life, respecting them, doing what's right, acting with integrity. This is true virtue, and it begins with people.

eternal. Practically speaking, this meant prioritizing my marriage, caring for my children, and treating my employees with integrity.

A Great Marriage

I found the love of my life in a department store, McClellan's five-and-dime store in Altus, Oklahoma. Barbara Turner was a pretty, young part-timer in the stationery department. Neither of us will claim it was love at first sight. In fact, Barbara's first impression of me was that I was a little smart-aleck. Thankfully, that opinion gradually changed for the better. Barbara and I married young. I was a skinny nineteen-year-old just out of the Air Force Reserves. I had no college degree and had done nothing to distinguish myself. I lived in an easy-to-miss, red-clay town in the Midwest. But we knew that true joy does not come from what you have or don't have. It comes from serving the Lord and valuing what he values, which is people.

From our early years, Barbara and I set out to have a great marriage. Now, we're not perfect. Barbara will be the first to tell you that I'm not perfect. There are no perfect marriages or perfect families. But we have been married for almost sixty years (since 1961), and our love for one another grows as the years go by. We love each other, and we love our marriage.

Having a great marriage comes from listening to God's Word and doing what it says.

For example, Ephesians 4:29 tells us, "Let everything you say be good and helpful, so that your words will be an encouragement to those who hear them" (NLT). One of my secrets for having a great marriage is to never criticize my wife. She could give me a biscuit that looks like a hockey puck, but I would never criticize her for it. Criticism kills the joy of a marriage. I never criticize her in her dress, her looks, or anything because I know how much it would hurt her. No one wants to be criticized. Instead, I look for ways to encourage her.

Another principle I see from God's Word is to "serve one

another humbly in love" (Galatians 5:13). In marriage, serving means thinking about what the other person needs. It means not being selfish. When we serve one another, we consider each other in our daily decisions. We ask each other questions like, "Where would you like to eat?" or "What would you like to do?" These small, simple choices to put the other first go a long way in marriage.

Valuing the eternal means putting people first. We choose to do what's right in the everyday matters, choosing to follow God's Word by loving those he's placed in our lives.

Children Who Serve God

One of our goals was to raise children who served the Lord. As parents, we cannot control our children's decisions. Our children must decide for themselves whether they want to follow God. But through our actions as parents, we can choose how we represent Christ to our children. Our actions can either draw our children toward Christ or push them away from Christ. If you tell your children you're a Christian, and then they see you getting angry at them or criticizing your wife, that separates them from Christ. They associate your life with Christianity. If your actions don't line up with what you teach them, they will choose to reject Christianity if that's how Christians act.

Valuing the eternal means putting people first.

The first thing that will help your children is to show them a marriage they want to emulate. I often say that the best thing my parents ever did for me was love each other. Growing up, I saw how happy my parents were in their marriage, and I wanted to create the same sort of marriage in my life. I saw how they served the Lord through their lives and through their marriage, and I wanted the same for my life.

Second, my parents worked to instill certain qualities in me. They raised me to value the eternal above the temporal. By tithing when they had little to give, they taught me that God owns everything. Through hard work picking cotton and sacking groceries, they taught me the joy of banding together as a family and providing for one another. Those principles taught by my parents early on formed me into the man I am today.

In life, there will be many places where God tests you. Your kids are watching to see if you pass those tests of integrity. When I was raising children of my own, I made my marriage a priority, and my children saw that. I put my faith above my company. When the government passed a law that went against our faith, we risked losing our company in a lawsuit. We chose to stand up for our beliefs, no matter the cost. We chose to value people (in this case, the unborn), even if it meant losing our company. My children saw those decisions to live by what was right. When you live out your faith, you pave the way

> The first thing that will help your children is to show them a marriage they want to emulate.

for your children to follow Christ. If they see you putting people first, no matter the cost, they will likely choose to do the same.

Our Ethics Matter

Our relations with businesspeople—bankers, coinvestors, competitors, suppliers—have also been affected by our faith-based commitment to integrity. We say we intend to treat them forthrightly and respectfully, to observe the golden rule of treating others as we would like to be treated.

Question: Is this only what we intend, or does it actually happen?

It does happen, and I could give dozens of examples. If a supplier short-ships something that Hobby Lobby has ordered, we will, of course, point it out: "We ordered 100 cases of those Christmas ornaments, but you delivered only 92." However, what happens if they mistakenly delivered 106? I have called company owners to say, "Hey, we just got your shipment, but instead of a shortage, there's a 'longage.' You sent us more than what the invoice says." They can hardly believe their ears.

"Nobody has ever done this before!" they tell me.

Well, we do, because it is right.

If a supplier's representative makes an appointment to see one of our buyers and present his or her product line, I have instructed our team to be present and on time. It is not respectful for the representative to travel halfway across the state and then be told by the receptionist, "Oh, sorry. Jim's not going to be able to see you today—something came up."

If an agreement to purchase is made, the deal needs to be straightforward and clear: a given product for a given price (hopefully, a very good price!) by a certain date. Keep it simple. Do not go back later with "Oh, by the way" adjustments or requests for favors, additional discounts, and so on. The supplier needs to earn a living too.

Just so everyone was clear, I wrote up a sign that hangs on the walls of our interview rooms:

NOTICE TO VENDORS

It is Hobby Lobby policy that employees or owners
will not receive any gifts of any value from vendors.
Except for rare occasions, employees will not
accept dinner engagements, as they will be
with their families during the evening.
Hobby Lobby owners and buyers will pay
their share of lunches. Any gift received by
anyone will be returned to the sender.
Any violation of this policy will jeopardize the relationship
between Hobby Lobby Stores, Inc., and the vendor.
We thank you in advance for your cooperation.
David Green, CEO

My point here is that favors and kickbacks are not to be
considered. If a vendor has to slide something extra under the
table to a buyer, it inevitably drives up the vendor's price on
the product, which can only hurt my company. I'm told that
one-third of all corporate failures are related not to external

factors but to internal corruption. I don't ever want that to happen at Hobby Lobby.

> Whether it is in your marriage, your parenting, or your work ethic, integrity always wins.

The same goes for any kind of negotiation with a business partner. We need to be people of our word. It is possible to be smart and fair at the same time.

I hope that the decisions my family made will inspire others to lock down the core values that will define them and the next generation. Putting people before profit is always the right choice.

Even if valuing people means giving up a chance to earn a profit, it is always worth it. Whether it is in your marriage, your parenting, or your work ethic, integrity always wins.

Consider All the Blessings You've Been Given

The greatest blessings are the
ones that can never be lost.

*Not a lot of people know this, but I don't use a computer. I
don't have one at my desk. I also don't carry a cell phone. At
work, people can call me on a regular phone, and when I'm
out of the office, Barbara is with me, and she carries a phone. I
laugh a little bit at that, but I want to use technology instead of
having it use me. At Hobby Lobby, I consider us to be techno-
logically advanced, and I know how to get all the reports I need.*

*I also don't carry an iPad, but I do carry a "MyPad," a
little black book that I always have tucked inside my back
pocket. I go through these notebooks quickly enough that my*

daughter, Darsee, bought them for me in bulk. The cover of each one says, "My Dad's a Superhero!" In my MyPad, I write down some of the big goals or projects I'm working on. I've found that if I write it down, it gets done. That might mean getting up in the middle of the night to write down a new thought when it comes to me.

In the MyPad, I also write down the big things that I'm praying about. That list reminds me to keep praying. Sometimes prayer requests stay on the list for years, transferred from one notebook to the next. But God always answers my prayers. And when he answers a particular prayer, I cross it off my list as a reminder of his faithfulness. My MyPad is my little book of gratitude.

While my parents may not have been rich as the world defines it, they taught me the meaning of true blessings—blessings that went beyond what could be seen.

What do we mean when we talk about being blessed? In our culture, blessings are usually interpreted as financial blessing. As I tell stories about my parents' faithfulness in tithing and serving the Lord, and how he blessed them for it, people have said to me, "Well, your family was pretty poor to be considered blessed." Certainly, finances can be part of God's blessing. And in that sense, you could say that if my parents were not rich, God had not blessed them. But I don't think that's the case. Having money does not equal being blessed. Money can actually be a curse if it is not handled the right way. As I've met with CEOs of companies, I've seen it as a curse more than I have seen it as a blessing.

I have met plenty of billionaires whom I would not consider blessed. They have money, but some of them are miserable. Their families are broken. They do not have joy. Judging from their lives, money is not where true blessings are. True blessings are different from what the world sees.

Blessings go far beyond money. If you consider the blessings in other areas, my family was immensely blessed:

Family.

Friends.

Talents.

Freedom.

Education.

I could go on. I'm sure you could too. As I grew up in a family that loved and served the Lord, I discovered what true blessings are. The blessings God promises go far beyond money.

The Blessing of Work

As I mentioned earlier, since my dad pastored small congregations in rural America, our family didn't have a lot of money. We usually lived in a two-bedroom house. With five siblings, that meant my younger brother and I often made do with a rollaway bed in the kitchen. We never had a car. Our parents assured us that we each had two good feet to get us where we needed to go. Generous cousins frequently sent second-hand clothes, so my parents had to provide only underwear and socks for us. The people in our churches supplemented our meager income with weekly "poundings."

> Having money does not equal being blessed. Money can actually be a curse if it is not handled the right way.

Poundings were times during our church services when the faithful brought vegetables, fruit, and other food—often by the pound, hence the name—to the altar to help fill their pastor's pantry that week. Even with this generosity, we often went weeks without seeing meat on the table. Believe me, I learned early the difference between wants and needs.

Growing up without much, we learned to appreciate the closeness of one another. We were family, and we were together.

I remember years when my family needed a new piece of

furniture, and we would all pull together, go to the cotton fields, and pick cotton. I was seven or eight when my mother took a burlap potato sack, sewed a shoulder strap on it, and gave it to me as a bag for picking cotton. All eight of us went out—my parents, my four older siblings, one younger sibling, and I—to pick cotton together.

In the fall of the year, we would go out multiple times. After picking cotton, we would pool our money to provide a piece of furniture for the family. In addition to picking cotton, my siblings and I would come alongside the family however we could. My brothers and I would sack groceries. My sisters would wait tables.

As we worked together, it gave us a work ethic and a family connection. We were all working together for the same benefits. In all of the cotton picking, table waiting, and grocery sacking, we had a sense of gratitude and excitement. We were able to help our family financially. We were all working for the family. It was very unselfish because we knew it wasn't about us individually. Through my child-hood, growing up without much, we learned early how to count our blessings.

The Blessing of Generosity

I believe that God has placed us on this earth to work, to earn, and to care for those he has entrusted to us. Yet I also believe that we are put on this earth to give, to devote ourselves to a radical brand of generosity that changes lives and leaves a legacy.

When God first spoke to Abraham, he promised, "I will bless you; I will make your name great, and you will be a blessing" (Genesis 12:2). The blessing came so Abraham could pass it on. To paraphrase God's words to the patriarch Abraham, we are blessed so that we can be a blessing. The blessing carries a purpose that goes beyond ourselves, and even beyond this lifetime.

Today our children and even grandchildren are living out generosity. My son Mart has brought together several different Bible translation agencies to work on completing a Bible translation in every language within fifteen years. There are approximately six thousand languages in the world. Of those languages, two thousand have a Bible, two thousand are in the process of getting a Bible translated, and two thousand have no Bible translation work started. Mart's goal is to have a completed Bible in every language by 2033. My other son, Steve, has had a heart to build a Bible museum, and last year the Museum of the Bible opened in Washington, DC. Deciding to build the museum and putting it together was a long journey, which he and his wife, Jackie, shared about in their book, *This Dangerous Book*.[2]

> Blessing carries a purpose that goes beyond ourselves, and even beyond this lifetime.

And even our grandchildren are living out their adventures serving the Lord. Danielle is working for the Museum of the Bible; Tyler is involved with Salt and Light Leadership Training; Lauren and her husband, Michael, are in seminary; Brent has created movies for ministries . . . I could go on about each of my grandchildren, but I don't have room. As the apostle John wrote, "I have no greater joy than to hear that my children are walking in the truth" (3 John v. 4). Although he was talking about spiritual children, I believe the same joy applies to our actual children, and to grandchildren too! What a blessing to see each of them serving the Lord in their own unique way.

The Blessing of Faith

I'm grateful for the life my family lived when I was a boy. I am the son of two people whose feet were firmly planted in this world and yet who kept their eyes and hearts fixed on the world to come. A deep and unshakable faith in Jesus Christ flowed from my parents and filled our home. It was their lifeblood. Mom and Dad actually met at the same tent meeting where my father went to the altar to receive salvation—and my grandfather and my mother were the ones preaching at the time!

God has given many blessings: family, friends, freedom, education, a home, and many more. But even if I were to lose it all, I would still have the greatest blessing. I would still have Christ, and so I would still have everything. His death, resurrection, and gift of eternal life are by far the greatest blessings I could ever receive. Beyond Christ, everything else is just frosting. When I consider all of the blessings I've been given, it's hard for me not to pause and thank my Lord and my God. His heart is generous. His blessings are wide and rich.

> Beyond Christ, everything else is just frosting.

STEP 5

Develop a Vision
for Generosity

Every journey requires a destination.

*My friend Bill told me a great story about a woman he knew
named Leah Belle. She lived in the hill country of Colorado.
She and her husband were some of the first settlers to the
area, and they farmed the land. Sometimes the rains came,
and sometimes the droughts lingered. There were seasons of
plenty, and seasons where the snow would never seem to end.
They managed to carve a life and a living out of that land.*

*As the years crept along, Leah Belle and her husband
could no longer farm their four hundred acres. She fretted
over what to do with the land. One day, sitting on the front
porch of her house and gazing over the four hundred acres,*

Leah Belle found the Lord speaking to her: "Leah Belle, you are like the dog in the barn—you can't eat the hay but you won't let the cattle eat it either." She sensed clearly that this was God's direction. She decided to give up the land to a ministry, which in turn sold it and used the proceeds to further their mission.

"Now when I look up at that land," Leah Belle said, "I see people from every tribe and nation who call upon the name of Jesus!"

That's a vision for generosity, and that story inspires me. I realize that even if Hobby Lobby could one day be the largest company in the world, I would say, "So what?" There's got to be a larger purpose. I dream that one day we can translate the Bible into every language and spread the gospel to every person who has never heard it. That vision keeps me going.

At the core of any meaningful life and legacy has to be a vision for generosity, an understanding of what it means to be a blessing for others. The value of giving to church, to missions, to people must first be modeled, then taught so that the next generation embraces generosity as their calling. Once a person embraces a concept such as generosity as their own, then it's much easier to understand the responsibility attached to it.

My journey into generosity has shown me two important things, among others. First, generosity has a starting point. You don't just wake up one day and—*poof!*—you're generous. It begins with a decision to steward your resources with a heavenly mind-set. Second, generosity depends not on how much money we have but on the posture of our hearts. Too often we think of generosity as the sharing and giving of money. But that's a shallow definition. Generosity goes much deeper.

Generosity can start ever so small, but eventually have massive impact for God's kingdom.

A Note on Perspective

In his excellent little book *The Treasure Principle*, Randy Alcorn gives a vivid word picture about our perspective on generosity:

> Imagine you're alive at the end of the Civil War. You're living in the South, but you are a Northerner. You plan to move home as soon as the war is over.
>
> While in the South, you've accumulated lots of Confederate currency. Now, suppose you know for a fact that the North is going to win the war and the end is imminent. What will you do with your Confederate money?
>
> If you're smart, there's only one answer. You should immediately cash in your Confederate currency for U.S. currency—the only money that will have value once the war is over. Keep only enough Confederate currency to meet your short-term needs.[3]

Alcorn reminds us that our earthly currency has a time limit. Upon Christ's return or upon our death, all our money, as well as our possessions, will be worthless. Alcorn admits there's nothing wrong with money, "as long as you understand its limits." When we understand the temporary nature of this world and all that is in it, it should radically alter how we manage our resources, and our money in particular.

I don't know about you, but I don't want to get caught sitting on stacks of worthless money or heaps of meaningless possessions or mountains of unused resources. I want to put as much as I can into forms that will last for eternity.

Ninety Is Greater Than a Hundred

My journey begins in the cotton fields of my youth, learning the importance of tithing. I count myself fortunate to have received this message early and consistently from my parents. From the first dollar I made picking cotton as a grade-schooler, I was taught to give God 10 percent. Our family took Jesus literally when he said, "It is more blessed to give than to receive" (Acts 20:35).

> Generosity can start ever so small, but eventually have massive impact for God's kingdom.

My mother was particularly devoted to tithing. I remember when someone from the church brought our family some food—say, a bag of potatoes or some corn—Mother immediately calculated the market value of the gift so she could tithe 10 percent. If I heard her say it once, I heard her say it a thousand times: "Honour the LORD with thy substance, and with the first-fruits of all thine increase" (Proverbs 3:9 KJV).

My parents taught us to obey that verse faithfully. As I was growing up, I'd hear my dad say, "Ninety is greater than a hundred."

I remember asking him, "What do you mean by that?"

He replied, "Ninety percent with God is more than a hundred percent without him."

Generosity: God's Fuel for the Entrepreneur

Let me say again what I believe with all my heart. In all the world there are only two eternal things—the Word of God and the souls of people. All else is fleeting. Remember Randy Alcorn's story, shared earlier? To invest in eternal things is the most important thing we can do with our lives, our energies, and our resources. It's vital in our personal lives, and in our business ventures, that our perspective remains eternal rather than temporal.

At Hobby Lobby, we have chosen to be a company that gives. Naturally, the amount we give has gotten progressively larger over the years as the company has expanded. I don't begrudge one nickel of it. We've set out to work with organizations that tell people about Christ, from global ministries such as Every Home for Christ to our local City Rescue Mission.

> To invest in eternal things is the most important thing we can do with our lives, our energies, and our resources.

My personal faith directs my efforts and fuels my passion for generosity. Since I believe there's a real heaven and a real hell, I want to direct as many people toward heaven and away from hell as I can. I want them to know the peace that's available through knowing Christ. God has given us the resources and the partnerships to reach them. I truly believe there will be millions of people in heaven because of this effort.

For me, the question is not, "Why would we use our profits for this?" It is rather, "Why *wouldn't* we use our profits for this?" If we don't use Hobby Lobby's earnings to touch people for the Lord, I really don't see the reason for me to be in business at all.

As with anything in life, we are not going to do it unless we see the purpose. We are not going to be generous unless we see why we're being generous. We will not be generous until we see the impact our generosity can have on others.

Sitting in church on a Sunday night back in 1997, Barbara and I learned about an outreach to the world's children called Book of Hope. Today it is called OneHope. A speaker that night explained how for just thirty-three cents, they could print and deliver a sixty-four-page color booklet that told the story of Christ's life, death, and resurrection in terms understandable to a child. He said they had invitations to do this in many schools around the globe using volunteer teams.

> If we don't use Hobby Lobby's earnings to touch people for the Lord, I really don't see the reason for me to be in business at all.

I went up after the service and talked to the speaker, inviting him to visit me in my office in Oklahoma City and share details. Eventually, he arranged for Book of Hope's president, Bob Hoskins, to come see me. The meeting went well. I got answers to my questions, and I was impressed with what this program could do to impact the youth of the world. I agreed to make a contribution of $2 million.

Here's where it gets interesting. Bob had his meeting with me but did not tell his son Rob about it. Separately, but about the same time, Rob received a request from a missionary in the Philippines who wanted Rob to meet with the minister of education for their country. "I want to try to get the Book of Hope in all the Philippine high schools!" the missionary told Rob enthusiastically.

"How many kids would that be?" Rob asked.

"Six million."

Rob did the math in his head. How could they ever raise $2 million for just one country? Still, he agreed to fly to Manila for the meeting with the government official.

The day of the meeting came, and the missionary made his pitch to the minister of education. When the missionary was done, the minister of education became very serious. "We appreciate the United States and all you've done for our country," he said. "You helped us rebuild after World War II. We set up our system of education to follow your pattern. But when you took the Bible out of your schools in 1963, we followed suit. So I am denying your request, based on your own government's laws."

Up to that moment, Rob Hoskins had let the missionary do all the talking. But he felt agitated at the education minister's response and decided to jump in. "Sir," Rob responded, "do you know what has happened to our nation's youth since 1963?" He then reeled off statistics about the rise in violence, alcohol abuse, drugs, and teen pregnancy, and the drop in SAT scores.

Before long, the government official started commiserating with Rob! He told statistics of his own, which mirrored the American numbers. Then something odd happened. The official pushed himself back from his desk and called for his secretary. He said he wanted to dictate a letter of permission for the Book of Hope to be brought to every Filipino school child.

"Now, I'm going to put my name and my seal on this letter," he said to his two visitors. "Can you really make this happen?"

In that moment, Rob's brain thought, *There's no way!* But he opened his mouth and answered, "Yes, we can do it."

The missionary beside Rob almost fell out of his chair. Once outside, he turned worriedly to Rob and said, "Do you know what you just promised? What if you can't raise the money? You'll get on a plane tomorrow, but I have to stay here and live with these people!"

During a plane change in Tokyo on the trip home, Rob called his father in Florida. "I have good news and bad news," he announced. "The good news is that permission has been granted. We have an open door all across the Philippine school network. The bad news is that we need $2 million right away."

The father started laughing on the other end of the line.

"Don't fret, son," he said. "Remember that meeting in Oklahoma that I went to? I'm sitting here holding a check in my hand for $2 million!" Both men began to weep.

Since that day more than two decades ago, we've continued to partner with this strategic ministry. I love the impact they are making all around the world. Their vision is simple: "God's Word. Every Child."[4] Their financial model is equally clear: "Three for a dollar." Now, that's a concept a retailer can understand! Nearly every member of our family has traveled overseas with them and helped to pass out this life-giving book. We've all been enriched and stretched through the experience.

I tell this story not to boast about what Hobby Lobby has done, but to inspire you to see how God can use your giving. He is the one who coordinates each gift.

During my meeting in Oklahoma City with Bob Hoskins, I had no idea what amount their ministry would need. Bob had no idea either. But God knew. Through giving, we join God in his divine work. We get to peek behind the curtain and see how he uses our gifts to miraculously provide for others.

Another ministry we have been honored to partner with is Every Home for Christ, led by Dick Eastman. This ministry gives me great confidence because Dick and his wife, Dee, are great prayer warriors. I know that their ministry is bathed in prayer. I like Every Home for Christ because of their work in planting churches all around the world. They are going door-to-door handing out literature in 130 nations.

One time my son Mart was speaking in a country in Asia. He mentioned that Hobby Lobby had given to Every Home for Christ to help support the ministry's church-planting efforts in that country. At the service that evening, one of the other speakers leaned over to Mart and said, "You do know that some of these audience members are the fruit of your giving. Many of these came to Christ through Every Home for Christ."

> Through giving, we join God in his divine work.

Their lives were changed because of a gift we gave. Thousands of people like us have given to mission work. Sometimes we get to see the fruit of our giving, and sometimes we don't. Rarely do we get to randomly meet a person on the other side of the globe whose life was impacted by a gift we gave. But that service in Asia was a picture of what heaven will be like. We will get to meet all the people who came to Christ because of our small acts of obedience.

You'll only start being generous when you see how far your gift can go and the impact it can have for eternity.

STEP 6

Create a Plan for Generosity

Those who plan to give, do.

I'm blessed that my work at Hobby Lobby provides me with the opportunity to be out and about instead of stuck in an office. My days are often filled with visiting stores or being in the warehouse. I don't sit at my desk a lot. I have heard it said that the most important decisions are never made sitting behind a desk. As a result, I find myself walking frequently. I suppose that one of these days I could end up with a fitness watch just to see how many miles I walk a day.

But even with all that exercise, I still keep a little room right down the hall from my office. Some days I think of it as the torture room. It's where I keep my exercise equipment.

Sometimes I'll make time to get on that equipment. Sometimes I don't. But I know that if I don't plan on it, then I won't.

Giving is the same. You have to plan to give. Unless you plan to give, you won't give. If you want to live a life that money can't buy, it takes a plan. It takes intention.

My wife, Barbara, is good at planning to give. More than money, she gives her time and her creativity. Starting in 1990, she served for more than twenty years on the board for City Rescue Mission, helping the homeless here in Oklahoma City. And for the past twenty years, she has hosted a tea to raise money for the homeless. The first tea party began in 1999 as a small affair. She invited twelve ladies into her home as a fund-raiser. Now, two decades later, about eight hundred ladies come together for the annual "Hearts of Hope" tea fund-raiser. She buys a teacup for each guest and a teapot for each table, which the table host gets to take home. The ladies love to come. I think it's because Barbara is so down-to-earth; they just love her. Each year she raises hundreds of thousands of dollars. Over time, she has raised millions for the rescue mission.

This tea party did not start by accident. Barbara had a passion for helping the homeless in our city. She set about giving her time and creativity to create an event that would inspire others to give to the cause she cared about so deeply. It wasn't just a whim. It was calculated dedication, and she stayed faithful year after year.

That's how giving works. It takes planning.

You might be stuck trying to decide where to give your resources and how much to give. These are important considerations for us all at any age. I want to encourage you in your giving and perhaps ignite some ideas for you. It's important to set criteria when deciding which organizations to give to. Then you've got to decide on an amount and create a plan of action.

My hope is that what I say will inspire you, whether you're an early-stage entrepreneur, a married couple, a seasoned business owner, or a soon-to-be college graduate. So let your mind play a bit, and see whether God ignites your heart with the fire of generosity.

Set Your Criteria

As you might imagine, we've had to develop some criteria about where to place our gifts. There's no lack of people and organizations knocking on our door for help. Our criteria come out of what I said earlier about the biggest issue of all for us: eternal destiny. We base our giving decisions on whether the result will be some spiritual change in a person's life, directly or indirectly.

As Barbara and I taught our children to go beyond tithing by giving to additional organizations, we trained them to differentiate between good and great. We taught them to ask, "Is this going to matter a thousand years from now?" If not, it might be a good thing, but it's not a great thing. For example, it's a *good* thing to give food to a child who's hungry. But it's a *great* thing to also tell that child the truth that will affect his or her life for eternity.

We want to take a lot of the good things we do, like drilling wells overseas, and make them great.

> Let your mind play a bit, and see whether God ignites your heart with the fire of generosity.

Think of a scale from one to ten. Whenever people come to Christ, we consider that a ten. That's why I love organizations that lead people to Jesus. Training Christians to go out and lead people to Christ is a nine for me. That's the reason we got involved with several Christian colleges, for example. They're training students to go out into the world as lights for Christ. Those ministries fall under the category of "great."

On the other hand, the local Boy Scouts and the chamber of commerce are good causes, but neither is a nine on our list.

We don't mind supporting good things in our community, but this kind of giving is not the central reason we exist. We seek to invest God's profits in things that will make a real difference for eternity.

I've mentioned two new projects that are very exciting and reflect our giving criteria. One is called Every Tribe Every Nation (www.everytribeeverynation.org). Every Tribe Every Nation's goal is to get God's Word to every person on earth. The second big project is the Museum of the Bible (www.museumofthebible.org). This is a world-class museum in the heart of Washington, DC. Our decision to give to these organizations, among others, remains linked to our overarching mission to support organizations that are telling people about the love of Jesus Christ through God's Word. This is our primary criterion for giving.

> Ask, "Is this going to matter a thousand years from now?" If not, it might be a good thing, but it's not a great thing.

So, I've told you our focus. What's yours?

If you know it, pull out the notes app on your smartphone or open your journal and jot down your primary giving criteria. If you've not given it much thought, I encourage you to sit down with your family or business and pray about the direction God wants you to give. Rather than shotgunning resources all over the place, consider that there is much joy to be found in directing your efforts toward a certain area. It's exciting for us to see our efforts build into such a wonderful impact on the lives of so many folks.

Set Your Giving Amount

The ideas in this section can apply either to an individual or to a business owner. From a business perspective, the amount of money we have to give is, of course, dependent on the earnings of Hobby Lobby. A target these days is for us to give away roughly half of our earnings. The government actually allows people to deduct up to 50 percent of their income each year; we are inclined to take advantage of that opportunity. We view it as wise stewardship to use all of the deduction we can, particularly because that increased giving level allows us to see more impact in the world through our giving.

The other half of our profits, understandably, goes toward growing the business—starting up more stores, making infrastructure improvements, and investing in other profitable ventures. The better payoffs we get from these things, the more we can plow into giving toward God's work. Again, the point is not to enrich any of us personally. The point is to be generous with what God has given.

Touching a torch to your generosity is obviously not the way a lot of business owners think today. Even Christian business owners find this approach to giving challenging. The reality is our collective national thought concerning generosity has shifted. Our financial planning advisor wrote not long ago in the *Christian Research Journal,* "The facts tell us that we've fallen short in our teaching and theology of money. The facts tell us that the largest givers in our history, the World War II Generation, are heading toward death and retirement and will be replaced by a generation of non-givers. The facts tell us that the current social and political climates don't bode well for giving."[5]

We are determined not to let the fire of generosity die out at Hobby Lobby. As long as God sees fit to prosper this company, we're going to keep giving back to God's work. Naturally, we want this God-given purpose to live in the next generation. This is part of the legacy we want to leave, not only in the amount of money we have generated (seen legacy), but in the commitment to give as God gives (unseen legacy), a commitment that we believe has led to all of our wealth in the first place.

> Don't underestimate the power of making a plan and writing it down.

We believe that if we can lead in the way that we give,

then we can inspire people from all walks of life to take up the mantle of generosity.

Generosity is about more than money. A generous spirit shapes us as individuals. We live with a perspective that differs from that of our consumer-driven society. A generous spirit affects how we use our time, those we seek to help in our community and abroad, and how willing we are to serve in our church gatherings. We want to display Jesus' character in how we give and inspire others to be generous too.

STEP 7

Talk About Money
with Your Children

What you know, you can change.
What you don't know controls you.

I'm aware of an older man who, having grown up in the Great Depression, has always kept financial matters close to the vest. He has built quite a net worth, with a variety of assets. But he still lives in fear of running out—a holdover from his childhood. He hasn't invested in technology. He doesn't use technology in the business, and he still keeps a six-days-a-week work schedule.

His kids work in the business and haven't gone out to seek other jobs. They assume they'll inherit the business someday. Yet nothing has ever been said about this. They are

using up their most productive years waiting for "someday."
Meanwhile, Dad keeps showing up at the office every day in
a suit and tie. He may live to be a hundred—who knows?

How much better it would be for everyone if this man
would talk to his family and make his plans known. How
much better for expectations to be communicated. It is some-
thing we all have to make a priority. If a child or grandchild
doesn't understand our reasoning, get to the bottom of it.
Communicate! Preserve the relationship at all costs. Be fair.
These steps will help the baton pass safely down the line.

Barbara and I have been far from perfect parents. In fact, we could write a book about all we've done wrong. But if there's one thing we've done right, it's that we've talked about financial issues with our children. From our children's earliest days, they knew that we expected them to earn what they made. That work ethic has carried over to today. Our children and our grandchildren are all workers, and that's something we are proud of.

We've also talked about the fact that Hobby Lobby belongs to God. It's not ours. We get to enjoy the fruit from the tree, but we can't touch the tree. That conversation helps us all to understand that God is our source. We are part of something bigger than ourselves, and we never want to put the rights of one individual over another. We are better when we work together for the greater goal. And we are better when we keep talking about the things that matter. Certainly, the financial life is something important to all of us and deserves attention in our conversation.

One of the great needs in families is to talk with one another about money and the responsibility it brings. I believe this is a rule of thumb. No matter what tax bracket you call home, you must *talk* about money. Talking about money with our children helps establish a clear understanding of how money works—how to spend it, save it, and pass it on.

In too many wealthy families, money is almost a hush-hush

topic. We all know money is a necessary part of life, but it feels too personal to bring up. This leaves room for assumptions and misunderstandings, which can result in bad planning and hurt feelings.

Talking about money is important because it helps set expectations. For the Green family, there is no free ride. We talk about money and also what it means to earn money. From the start, as Barbara and I raised our family, we wanted them to know what the Bible says about money. The Bible has a lot of negative things to say about money. It cautions us about the danger of materialism. Jesus warned, "It is easier for a camel to go through the eye of a needle than for someone who is rich to enter the kingdom of God" (Matthew 19:24). However, the Bible also has positive things to say about money. Proverbs 14:24 says, "The wealth of the wise is their

> One of the great needs in families is to talk with one another about money and the responsibility it brings.

crown, but the folly of fools yields folly." Money is a tool that can be terrible or wonderful, depending on whether we approach it with wisdom. We wanted our children to know the full picture regarding money.

The Importance of Giving

Barbara and I never debated whether to tithe on our modest paycheck when we got married. We believed that if we honored God in this way, he would bless us—maybe not financially, but in any number of other ways. When the children came along, we taught them the same principle.

As soon as they could count to ten, we taught them about tithing. If they received a small gift of money for their birthday or Christmas, we would talk to them about giving a tenth of the gift to church. I remember well when Mart and Steve began working in our kitchen, gluing picture frames. They carefully computed the tithe on their tiny income and then joyfully put it in the offering plate on Sundays. They were only nine and seven years old when we started our business, but they already understood that even if you were earning only seven cents for making picture frames, 10 percent went to God. They never complained about this sacrifice. They were grateful to do it.

To this day, Mart says, "I never thought about *not* tithing. It was just what we did in our house. It was our starting point with regard to money."

We also shared with our children the story of my parents tithing from produce. Many members of my dad's congregation were not rich. When their parishioners paid for services my dad would perform, if they did not have the money, sometimes they would bring vegetables from a garden. As I mentioned earlier, my mother would calculate the value of these "poundings" and pay a tithe on them back to the church. None of this was done out of obligation. My mother and dad loved to give. They knew God would bless them in that, and they received greater blessings than financial blessings.

The value of giving to God was embedded in our children from the earliest days.

We also wanted to make sure that their vision for generosity went beyond the tithe. We taught them to live their lives focused on what would be eternal. You can spend your life either on the eternal or on things that aren't going to matter.

If a generous life is one that leaves a legacy, we would be remiss not to include our children in conversations about giving. Now that our children are older, we practice generosity as a family. We meet together regularly to discuss our giving opportunities and decide where to give. Each request is viewed through our two criteria of the eternal: Will it advance God's Word? Will it save a person's soul?

> You can spend your life either on the eternal or on things that aren't going to matter.

We involve the whole family in this process, both myself and Barbara, as well as our children. Our grandchildren have opened their own donor-advised fund and started their own quarterly meetings where they decide where to give as a family. Involving the younger generations in our decisions on where to give has been essential in passing on our value of generosity.

Earn Your Way

Barbara and I have not promised any of our family members a job at Hobby Lobby. We have said they are welcome to apply, with the understanding that they'll have to perform like anyone else. There's no "tenure" just for being a Green.[6]

I'm aware that some experts in the field of family business transition discourage the hiring of a family member right out of high school or college. Some consultants recommend that a relative ought to work somewhere else for at least two years before coming aboard. Still other consultants suggest three to five years in one or more jobs requiring competence, skill, and sustained performance, with at least one of those jobs lasting at least two years and resulting in at least one promotion. Only then do they recommend hiring the young person to work within the family business.

We haven't taken that route. Still, I wouldn't argue against it. I agree that it's important not to get into a rush or build expectations that haven't been justified by observation. We do our kids and grandkids no favors setting them up for failure.

The apostle Paul wrote to one church, "When we were with you, we gave you this rule: 'The one who is unwilling to work shall not eat'" (2 Thessalonians 3:10).

I happen to think this verse applies even to someone who has a large trust fund. God put us here to work. He invented work long ago in the garden of Eden. Even before the fall, Adam and Eve were given the assignment to take care of the garden—to cultivate what God had given them.

Work is not a curse. It is our calling. We should keep working as long as we're able.

Fred Smith Sr., a Texas business legend and board member

of several Christian organizations, taught a large Sunday school class at a major Dallas church. One day after class, a woman approached him with a prayer request. "Would you please pray for my son? He's done with college now, and he's just trying to find the will of the Lord for his life."

"Well, sure," said Smith, "I'll pray for him. What's he doing now? Is he working?"

"No, he's just taking some time off," the mother replied, "waiting for God to show him his will."

Next question from the teacher: "Is he eating?"

The woman looked puzzled as she answered, "Oh, yes. He's staying at our place for the time being."

> Work is not a curse. It is our calling.

"Okay, you go home and tell him he's already out of the will of God!" Smith replied with a grin. "The Bible says that if a man doesn't work, neither shall he eat. So he's already out of line with what God said."

I totally agree.

Take Care of What You Work For

Stewardship is simply taking care of what you have and what you work for. It's looking after the things we've been given.

As I've stated throughout this book, I simply don't believe that unearned money helps grow the kind of responsible, motivated, focused offspring we all desire. As a parent, I would tell my children, "The hardest thing for me is to not do something for you." I would see them struggling, and I wanted to step in and take over, but I knew they needed to learn on their own. When we really love our kids, we need God's wisdom to know how to help them handle money. We simply must raise kids and grandkids to be independent. Otherwise we make cripples out of them.

I don't want any family member to have a choice about whether to work. Every one of them needs to go to work. I will not take that incentive from them.

Our son Mart recalled, "In high school, I was disappointed that my dad wouldn't buy Steve and me a car. I did manage to get a car at age sixteen, thanks to the fact that I'd been working and saving since I was nine! Dad may have given me a little money for the purchase, but not much.

"It was 1977, and he took me to a car auction. I bought a banana yellow '73 Ford Mustang convertible, one of the last convertibles they made for a while. It looked cool, but it didn't turn out to be such a wise choice. With that rear-wheel drive, it was horrible on snow. I got rid of it fairly quickly, switching to a front-wheel-drive Honda."

> We simply must raise kids and grandkids to be independent. Otherwise we make cripples out of them.

Mart went on to make an interesting observation: "Looking around at my high school and college friends, I could just about tell you which ones had paid for their car themselves by how they drove it! You take better care of something you worked for."

One of our grandkids told me that his school friends made an interesting remark after seeing his older, high-mileage car:

"What's up? Are you on the outs with your family or some-thing?" These friends assumed that any of the Green clan would be provided with the newest and greatest. No, that isn't how it works.

God put Adam and Eve in the garden to work. God set up work as an institution before the fall. It is part of a perfect world he designed for us. Part of sin's curse was to make work difficult, but work itself is not a curse. Barbara and I have striven to instill a work ethic in our children and help them see work itself as one of God's blessings to us. A great deal of harm can be done by passing on wealth to children if it takes away a healthy incentive to work.

Barbara and I love our family and want to share with them. We'll probably leave each of them a modest amount in our will, but certainly not enough to float a lifestyle. We never want to be viewed as our grandchildren's heroes. We stand behind their own parents, who carry the primary responsi-bility to shape their children. We don't want to usurp their parents' authority and influence.

If we ever think about doing something financially for one of the grandchildren, we consult with the parents first. We'll say, for example, "What if we paid for a third of their college if you, the parents, pay a third and the kid earns a third?" We try to stay in the shadows.

There is one thing we've arranged that might be considered a family perk. We've created an investment fund in Hobby Lobby for any family member who wants to open an account. Our children and grandchildren can put their money into the company and earn 8.5 percent, which is better than savings accounts are paying these days.

Most of our grandchildren have taken advantage of this. So they can say they are minority investors in the family business. Yet the capital is money they've earned themselves, not anything that was handed to them.

The bottom line is this: no family member, of whatever generation, must ever view Hobby Lobby as his or her source of well-being for all of life. God is our source! He is more than enough for all of us. If we keep our eyes on him and stay lined up with his purposes, we'll be all right. We can confidently go about our daily work, knowing God is our provider and accepting his invitation to do the job he's provided for us.

Talk About Inheritance

Remember the story I shared about my friend who grew up in the Great Depression and has not yet told his children whether they will inherit any of his business? His children are spending their most productive years waiting for a "someday" that may never come. Don't let that happen to your family. Your children and grandchildren need to know what to expect regarding their inheritance. This is typically a taboo topic, but it bears bringing up.

When I realized that God owned Hobby Lobby, this changed the way the company would be passed down. I decided not to split up the business but instead to keep it together in a trust. Unfortunately, we had already made estate-planning arrangements that gave each family member control of his or her own slice of the wealth. This meant that we had to engage in long conversations and planning sessions to create the new trust that would supersede and absorb all previous trusts. Everyone had to sign off on canceling the old and installing the new.

> No family member, of whatever generation, must ever view Hobby Lobby as his or her source of well-being for all of life. God is our source!

We finally got to that place during a family meeting in November 2011. All my children and grandchildren agreed with the new plan and were willing to put it in writing. At the same time, we worked to hammer out our values and our mission, as well as our philosophy of inheritance. Those hours of discussion—crafting language, working for agreement in our goals, and ultimately embracing a plan for the use of wealth—brought our family together and solidified us in a way I never had dreamed. We became strong, unified, filled with common vision, and eager for the future.

Eventually, someone will talk with your children about what you are passing on. It's simply a matter of whether you will be present for that conversation or not.

I started my career working retail, stocking shelves. I got married and started a family. I've lost sleep wondering about the future of my wife and kids. Now I'm entering the area of the baton exchange, and I want to do it well. I want my children and grandchildren to grow up understanding that generosity begins with an attitude that extends into every aspect of life, not just money. I want them to understand that today begins *their* legacy. Because if there's one thing I've discovered, it's that true wealth encompasses all of life.

Money does not last. It can be squandered. It can corrupt. It can blind you to what matters most in this world. But the values we ingrain into our family last beyond death. I want my kids and their kids to see how I used my gifts and God's blessings to serve others, not myself.

Give Even When It Seems Impossible

You won't know whether you can
out-give God until you try.

Sometimes after I speak at an event, audience members will come up and tell me they just can't give like Hobby Lobby. I smile and tell them to give right where they are at. It might be easy to think that because you don't have a lot, you shouldn't give. But God never counts the amount, only the heart of the giver.

One such man attended one of our CEO groups, and he came away encouraged and challenged to increase his giving, even while still trying to grow his business and get out of debt. His situation is like that of so many people I know—still try-

*ing to pay bills, deal with debt, and take care of family needs.
But this man resolved to increase his giving by 1 percent each
year. Each year he's kept to that resolution. It's allowed him
to manage his family and business situation while at the same
time be faithful to what God has called him to do.*

*That's the power of a calling. It's usually a gentle nudge
more than it is a bright light on the road to Damascus. Our
challenge is to obey that nudge.*

Growing up, I always felt like the black sheep of the family. I was the only one out of my siblings not to go into full-time ministry. This feeling remained until 1979.

In its early years, Hobby Lobby did not give corporate donations. I said to myself back then, *Maybe later. I need to use every dollar now to grow this business . . . so we can give more down the road.*

Then, in 1979, I was attending a large convention of my

denomination in Tennessee. Missionaries from all over the world gave presentations on their work. I paid close attention, remembering how my mother had always given special care and effort to funding foreign missions. As I flew home after the meetings, I was looking out the airplane window when something unusual happened. It seemed a quiet voice inside of me said, *"You need to give $30,000 for literature."* During the convention, one of the speakers had talked about the need for more printed material in his particular field. His words came back to me as I sat on that plane.

My first reaction to the words I sensed in my heart was that $30,000 was far too much money to consider. The company wasn't nearly big enough to afford that amount. We had only four stores. *No,* I concluded. *This is impossible!*

Yet the impression wouldn't go away.

God, I don't have $30,000, I silently prayed. *But you're serious about this, aren't you?* It was just then that I had an idea. *Well, I suppose I could write four checks for $7,500 each, and post-date them a month apart for the next four months.*

I sat there pondering this option. Then I did some calculating. Maybe this would work after all.

When I reached home, I wrote the four checks. I then put them in an envelope, took a deep breath, prayed that I could make good on them, and mailed them to Tennessee.

When the church official on the other end called to acknowledge my gift, he made an intriguing comment. "The day your letter was postmarked," he said, "was the very day that four African missionaries had a special prayer meeting for literature funds. Looks like God answered their prayer!"

Something clicked inside me at that moment. My long-standing uneasiness about not going into the ministry like all my brothers and sisters went away. It settled permanently inside of me that God had a purpose for a businessman. He had called me. He had blessed me. There must be a role for people like me in the work of the kingdom of God.

I could tell more stories of wonderful partnerships. From the track record of corporate earnings that is now building year by year, it seems to me that God is smiling on this philosophy of giving. Hobby Lobby has retired all long-term debt, and our profits have continued to grow, even throughout the last recession.

Other business owners may say to me, "Well, that's nice. You're riding high these days, so no wonder you can be generous. My situation is different, however. My industry is struggling, and I'm barely hanging on. I can't afford to give."

My reply is, "This is exactly the time to start

> It settled permanently inside of me that God had a purpose for a businessman. He had called me.

giving!" God will notice your heart. To commit yourself to his purposes can get you up and out of your struggle. I know this doesn't sound logical, but in God's eternal economy, it is true.

There's a phrase common in some Christian circles that goes, "You can't out-give God." I tossed around that phrase myself more than once. Then, about twenty years ago, God seemed to say to me, *"Well, you haven't really tried, have you?"* That really brought me up short.

I shared this with other family members. I told them, "I think we need to do something different. I think we're supposed to test God and see if we can out-give him." I asked the family to pray about it.

I didn't give them any specific amounts or suggestions. I simply asked them to consider it. After that conversation, my oldest son, Mart, came to me with a plan for giving. It was exactly the same plan that I had been thinking about but hadn't told them yet. Clearly the Lord was leading us. We agreed that Hobby Lobby needed to launch out into whole new ventures of giving.

The plan was to give the largest amount we had ever given, and to give it over the next six months. The following six months, we would add that same amount and give double. We would keep adding that same amount indefinitely, every six months. We would continue this pattern thereafter. With that giving pattern in mind, Mart and I calculated where we would be in five or six years. We looked at what seemed an astronomical number and said, "This is impossible."

Well, it's been more than twenty years, and right now we're actually ahead of that schedule. God has proven faithful. We're now giving at a level I previously thought impossible, and we're still going! The more this business gives, the more God blesses us to keep giving.

> The more this business gives, the more God blesses us to keep giving.

Like a lot of families, we started with giving to our church. Then we expanded to mission agencies. God keeps bringing us causes bigger than ourselves. Even as the projects grow in size and scope, our business has kept growing. We truly cannot seem to get ahead of him.

It's so easy to rationalize not giving.

"We're in a recession."

"My business is struggling."

"We just had our first child."

"I have a mountain of school loans."

"I'm about to retire and need the funds."

The list goes on. In my own journey, I've discovered that the timing of generosity reveals your heart to God. That step of writing the check or hitting the "donate" button online can seem daunting. But it all comes down to trust. Do I really trust that God is the same God who stayed Abraham's hand from slaughtering his son and provided a ram in the thicket for the sacrifice? If my answer is yes, then that carries consequences. Good ones too.

> When to give? I humbly suggest *always.*

It means that as a consequence of God's provisional faithfulness, I can take joy in giving even in hard times. Oftentimes God just wants us to take the first step. It can be as simple as making a plan to get out of debt or a plan to support a missionary family for a decade. It's the first step. Once we commit, I've found that God is quick to reveal himself in that endeavor.

When to give? I humbly suggest *always*.

We give with joy in our hearts.

We give out of our humble circumstances.

We give out of our wealth.

It doesn't matter whether we give out of wealth or humble circumstances. God can't wait for us to step into the joy of generosity. We just need to trust him and take that first step.

As I consider my giving journey, the thing that has surprised me the most is how much joy it has brought me. I never could have imagined the people or the places that I would see. I never could have imagined all the lives that would be impacted. That brings me joy and peace that is hard to quantify.

My son Mart likes to quote Chip Ingram, who says,

"Generosity is a gateway into intimacy with God."[7] And that's the big thing: God is a giver. We were made in his image, and when we act like him, we become like him.

In Hebrews 12:2, the writer said of Jesus, "For the joy set before him he endured the cross." Joy and giving go together. I think the most satisfied and joyful person in heaven will be Jesus as he looks around at all those he has redeemed by giving his life.

Let me take my plea to you. Take God at his Word. Test him. I'm convinced that if you take a step and keep moving forward on the adventure of giving, there is no way that you'll be disappointed.

STEP 9

Create a Family
Legacy Plan

Passing on wealth means passing on all forms of wealth.

Family legacy. People might hear those words and think it only applies to those with money. Yet I think back to my mom and dad's legacy. We surely didn't have a lot, but my fondest memories are of our family gathered around the dinner table, laughing and sharing the stories of our day. Those were good days. As I mentioned earlier, we traveled a lot, since every two years my dad was assigned to a new church. With frequent moves, it was hard to make friends, but we had each other.

I remember waking up late at night and hearing the prayers of my parents—earnest, heartfelt prayers. These were people who knew God and depended on him. I'm sure it must have been hard to raise six children on a meager income. It must've been hard to watch their children adjust to never-ending address changes. But they lived with a singular vision of souls won for Christ. All else paled in comparison. They passed down that singular vision to their children, and now I desire to pass it down to future generations.

My parents lived a life that money could not buy. They lived and left a great legacy, and they prove that a legacy need not include the financial. I'm hopeful that more and more families will take up this banner.

I never thought I'd see a day when three generations of Greens would be sitting around a table, discussing generosity. It does something to you deep inside to see your children and their children share the same values and heart for God. Not a day goes by that I don't thank God for this blessing.

All that you have read thus far in this book shows the blessing of God upon Hobby Lobby and the lessons of God for the Green family. These blessings and lessons make up our legacy. It's a legacy that arises from a pastor's home in some of the small towns of America. It was born of the prayers of my parents. It took flight as I fell in love with the retail business, married Barbara, and began a life with her of generosity in obedience to God. It was fashioned both in hard times and in seasons of blessing, in the valleys and on the soaring mountain peaks. Always, it was sustained by the God who owns Hobby Lobby and who ordains that the company be used for his purposes alone.

I believe with all my heart that these are the reasons— along with the good business sense God also gave us—that Hobby Lobby is as successful as it is. It was God's idea. It is God's company. It was only entrusted to the Green family. Our job has been to lead it to the best of our ability in a manner that honors Jesus Christ and touches as many lives as possible for eternity.

I want future generations to know the God who sustains us. I want them to hear the stories of how God has come through over and over, for both our family and our company, through the good times and the hard times. I want a legacy plan that leads to a united family whose legacy continues long after Barbara and I are gone.

The Dilemma

Now, before I continue, I understand that the idea of wealth transfer might sound a bit odd to some of you. But it's important to think about how we will transfer wealth from one generation to the next. If done incorrectly, a poorly handled wealth transfer can have disastrous results for a family. We need only to turn on the television or hop on the internet to see the monstrous effects great wealth can have on people who possess no moral compass, no compassion for others, and only a desire to get rich and stay rich. If no safeguards are in place, then the next generation will struggle to keep the family vision intact.

Keep in mind that wealth transfer is not just about money. In our Green family document, which I will share more about later, we define wealth as "intellectual, social, financial, and spiritual capital." In passing on a legacy to the next generation, I want to pass on more than just financial wealth. Proverbs says, "Wisdom is more profitable than silver, and her wages are better than gold" (3:14 NLT). If God values wisdom over financial wealth, we feel that it would be wrong, and even harmful to our family, to only pass on riches and not all the other wisdom God has given over the years.

Transferring wealth or the wisdom of a family vision from one generation to the next can be tricky. But it can be done successfully if a vision is in place. A vision for the Green family carries philanthropic, ethical, and spiritual implications. I believe it's the same for you.

How Wealth Can Divide

I found myself in crisis during the 1990s. You recall that I described having sleepless nights over the great weight of the wealth we were reaping from the company. It was the crisis that God answered by telling me that he owned Hobby Lobby.

That clear revelation solved a problem I was wrestling with in those days—finding the best way to transfer wealth to the next generation.

Beginning in the 1990s, Hobby Lobby made huge profits. Over the years, this has totaled billions of dollars. Every year now, I am listed on the *Forbes* magazine elite list, called the Forbes 400, the magazine's list of the wealthiest people in America. I have asked the Forbes people to keep me off of their list, but they refuse to listen. Still, my inclusion on this list will give you some sense of the great abundance God has given us by blessing Hobby Lobby.

The truth is that we are one of the most profitable companies in America. You can find larger companies. You can find better-known companies or companies that are more global. Yet you would be challenged to find a more profitable company than ours. This is all, of course, the blessing of God on what started as a frame-cutting operation in an Oklahoma garage.

I know a lot of this Hobby Lobby history may not seem as though it applies to you, but stick with me, and I promise I'll make it practical for you at the end.

When you have great wealth to manage, you will always have experts, financial managers, and advisors to help you with the task. This is as it should be, because no one should make decisions about such vast sums alone. The traditional wisdom among financial advisors is that a man of my wealth should create a legacy for his children by setting up a complicated system of trusts and corporate structures to minimize estate taxes, which can often run as high as 55 percent. The goal, to put it crassly, is to beat the IRS so that you have more to pass on to your heirs. So you create various trusts and legal structures that provide for the transference of wealth in such a way that the tax code allows you to avoid as many taxes as possible.

It is not a process for the fainthearted. It involves mountains of paperwork and armies of lawyers. Hours of discussion lead to lengthy explanations by experts, which are turned into documents to sign not once but a dozen times! The hope is that when it is all done, there is peace, since your family is provided for in abundance for years to come.

Barbara and I did as we were advised. We hired smart people and told them to use the wisest instruments and strategies possible. We did all that is usually done to pass wealth on to children and grandchildren. With all the planning we'd done, we should have been at peace. We should have breathed a sigh of relief and then never again had to trouble ourselves with such matters.

It didn't happen that way.

The truth is that I grew more and more uneasy. Something about the whole process didn't seem right to me. Odd as it may sound, I was troubled in my spirit, in my innermost being. It wasn't just that I mentally objected to what was happening. It was that something seemed out of line with God's will.

I couldn't sleep.

I thought about the matter constantly and probably wore Barbara out talking about it.

The traditional approach to passing on wealth to the next generation separated my unified Christian family by breaking up or passing down ownership to children, grandchildren, and great-grandchildren. I envisioned a few generations down that we could have hundreds of shareholders, each with his or her own interests. We were a family deeply committed to each other and to Christian purposes for the wealth we had been given. Yet the approach we had agreed to for transferring wealth broke up my family into individual pieces.

Under this traditional approach, it struck me that the aim was to promote the individual interests of hundreds of shareholders. Those shareholders could or would vote their interests instead of the larger family interests. That made me uncomfortable. It seemed to me that we needed to keep a united vision for our family. It doesn't matter if you're a wealthy business owner, a rookie entrepreneur, or a couple planning their family and the next five years—breaking up your family's vision is never a good thing.

The Importance of Family Vision

I was disappointed with what had been set in place for my family. Something had to change.

Bill High had some great advice at this point. Bill is a lawyer and an executive with The Signatry, a global Christian foundation. He first entered our lives as a financial advisor to Mart while Mart was producing the film *Beyond the Gates of Splendor*. Bill advised Mart about nonprofit law and offered numerous helpful solutions to challenges facing that project. This led to other roles for Bill in advising our family and company. His wisdom and easygoing manner made him perfectly suited for facilitating communication and creating consensus on many important matters.

At Mart's recommendation, I asked Bill to meet with our

family. He did, and very gently offered his observations about what was in place and what might be done to facilitate the management trust. The family seemed to trust him immediately. They asked if he could help us get through this critical transition. Bill agreed. I was grateful.

Bill spoke of taking a complicated and legalistic succession plan and remaking it into a family legacy plan. He spoke of it as a kind of constitution that would guide the family for generations. It would provide a family vision, a family mission, guiding values, a giving statement, prerequisites for being a member of the management trust, and finally, a wise plan for implementing all of this.

> It doesn't matter if you're a wealthy business owner, a rookie entrepreneur, or a couple planning their family and the next five years—breaking up your family's vision is never a good thing.

I found it easy to work with Bill. He enjoys fast-paced

conversations like I do, and he often showed up for our meetings with notes written out on a napkin—just like me. Perhaps more important, he has a story similar to mine of growing up in poverty, and he cares deeply about family. A bit less important but still helpful is that we share a love of Oreo cookies. And Bill seems to enjoy my lawyer jokes. Most lawyers don't. My grandchildren say that "you know you're family when Grandpa gives you a hard time."

What followed was a yearlong process of creating and embracing a Green family legacy plan. It wasn't without thoughtful, sacrificial, and sometimes painful decision-making. But we were committed.

We started with a series of family retreats. There were hours of discussion and exploring options. We even got into examining the personality type of each family member and learning about one another by using tools such as StrengthsFinder. We wanted to understand how each person is wired. Ultimately, this led to the development of our mission, vision, and values statements.

Our goal was to protect the company through the generations and to define who would manage that trust and for what purposes. And we did. We completed and signed the Green Stewardship Trust. Into this trust went the entirety of the Green family wealth.

The very first page of our document creating this trust establishes its purposes:

1. To honor God with all that has been entrusted to us
2. To protect, preserve, and grow the value of the Green Family Companies
3. To use the assets of Green Family Companies to create, support, and leverage the efforts of Christian ministries

By the second page, the document spells out how company donations will be dispersed. Perhaps the most revolutionary part of this endeavor is that our operative documents now direct that if the trustees ever get the notion to sell or liquidate more than 10 percent of the company, the rules for distribution are:

- 90 percent to Christian ministries
- 10 percent to a special-needs fund for family members who encounter some kind of urgent situation, such as a life-threatening disease

Nothing will go into the pockets of a shareholder or a trustee. This means it will do trustees little good to sell the company for personal gain. By insisting on this, we hope to keep Hobby Lobby on track as God's company, not ours. We want it to continue for decades, perhaps even centuries, as an ongoing source of financial fuel for God's work around the world.

The analogy of the tree is the best way to explain what we were trying to do. We think of Hobby Lobby as a strong, fruitful tree. Every season it bears another crop of, say, apples. If we take care of the tree—cultivating the soil around it, making sure it gets adequate water, spraying it as needed—it will yield wonderful fruit.

Anyone in the family, or even outside the family, is welcome to help take care of the tree. If they work diligently, they can receive a share of the results. If you are a good janitor at Hobby Lobby, you will get a bag of apples. If you qualify to be a vice president, you receive a whole bushel basket of apples.

Yet understand this: You cannot have the tree. It will never belong to you. It belongs to someone else. This is what we were trying to achieve with the Green Stewardship Trust, and I'm proud of its uniqueness and the way it honors God. But this basic concept is for everyone. The tree—your wealth and resources—belongs to God. And if your vision and mission reflect this truth, the tree will act as a safeguard for generations to come.

> We want [Hobby Lobby] to continue for decades, perhaps even centuries, as an ongoing source of financial fuel for God's work around the world.

As I mentioned at the start of this chapter, passing on financial capital is only one aspect of legacy. So in addition to creating the Green Stewardship Trust, we also created a document outlining our family's vision, mission, and values. Barbara, our children and their spouses, and I took a weekend to get away from home, away from work, and to focus on this second document. We spent a weekend at a resort to hash out who we want to be as a family. As we created this document, we tried to keep each aspect short and memorable. We focused on service for Christ, our love for the Lord, and our generosity toward others. We want God's Word to be the foundation of our family. For each value we included, we listed a scripture saying why that value matters.

Once we finished writing the document, we brought it to our next family meeting and presented it to the grandchildren.

"This is who we'd like to be," we told them. "Is there anything you want to change? Is this something you can accept?"

After some discussion, all ten grandchildren voted unanimously to accept it.

Creating the document united our family in ways I would not have imagined. Having our vision, mission, and values down formally in writing solidified us. Every member knows who we are as a family. Each has his or her own copy. It's hard for family members to feel like outsiders when they know who they are and what they are a part of. Are we a perfect family? No. Far from it. But we feel that creating the document has been a good step for us.

Celebrating Family

One November when we were a young family just starting out, I was working at TG&Y, the Wal-Mart of that era, headquartered in Oklahoma City. This was before we had ventured to start Hobby Lobby. TG&Y was scheduled to be open on Thanksgiving Day, which meant I would have to work that holiday instead of being home with our family. Well, Barbara wouldn't have it. For Barbara and me, family has always been the most important part of life, second only to serving the Lord.

Barbara called the president of TG&Y. He didn't answer. One of Barbara's many qualities is a powerful, gentle persistence, so she wasn't fazed. She just called again. And again. On about the seventh try, the president answered.

"I don't know a lot about business, but I know about family," Barbara told him. "This needs to be a day that you have for the family."

Despite Barbara's phone call, TG&Y remained open on Thanksgiving Day. A few years later, however, Barbara and I started Hobby Lobby, and we have closed the store for the holiday every year.

From our earliest days of marriage until now, family has always been a priority. We have tried to pass on that value, and one way we do that is by celebrating together. Once a month, we gather for birthdays. Right now there are thirty-nine of us, but that number keeps growing with grandchildren marrying and great-grandchildren on the way. In addition to our monthly celebrations, once a year we have an annual family get-together to just have fun and remember what God has done. During our time, different people will speak on a portion of our family document that has been meaningful to them over that past year.

Another way we celebrate family is by telling our stories so that they can be remembered. The Bible encourages this concept of telling stories to future generations. King David wrote in the Psalms, "Let each generation tell its children of your mighty acts; let them proclaim your power" (145:4 NLT). For us, telling our story to future generations includes putting our stories in today's technology, recording them in a way that can be preserved for future generations for years to come. We subscribe to a digital family archive service to record stories, pictures, and videos. Barbara and I have tremendous amounts of information in it. We've been videoed as we talk about what's important to us. We talk about ministries we've given to and different ways God has worked in our family. We talk about our marriage. We tell the story of how God took a $600 business we started in our garage and blessed it more than we could have dreamed. We also talk about the difficult times and how banks were going to foreclose on us. We want our children, grandchildren, and great-grandchildren to know what God has done.

Defining wealth as "intellectual, social, financial, and spiritual capital" changes the mind-set of creating a legacy plan. It encourages us to look at how we steward everything God has given.

So how are you managing your wealth in all its forms? How do you plan to transfer it to your children? Can you imagine the blessing of God to those who steward well the blessings they've been given? As we think about passing on our legacy, we think not only about what we are leaving behind, but also about what we will send ahead. We pass on a legacy, but we also look for ways to store up treasure in heaven.

STEP 10

Stockpile Treasure in Heaven

Legacy is not just what we leave
behind, but what we send ahead.

Growing up, my family did not have much artwork in our house. Money was tight, and our family got along with just the basics of life. Knickknacks, frills, and family photos were not to be found in our simple home. But there was one plaque my mother hung on the wall, and I have never forgotten its words. It was a short poem:

> Only one life, 'twill soon be past
> Only what's done for Christ will last.

In my teen years and for quite a few years into my adulthood, the words of that poem stirred up guilt inside me whenever I remembered them. Assuming the phrase "what's done for Christ" meant work done as a pastor with his flock, as an evangelist on the street corner, or as a missionary to remote tribes in Africa, I felt defeated because I knew those were things I could not do. Not until my late thirties did I discover the joy of giving to God's work and come to realize its lasting value.

Until recently, I had no idea that those lines were actually part of a longer poem with a very interesting story. It was written by the son of a wealthy British family, Charles Thomas (C. T.) Studd, who lived from 1860 to 1931. His father had made a fortune producing indigo dye in India. Charles and his brothers attended the best schools England could offer, first Eaton and then Cambridge, where Charles became, as some have called him, the Michael Jordan of cricket. Charles represented his country on the national cricket team and became a household name in Britain. He knew that when he turned twenty-five, he would inherit a large sum—some $25 million in today's dollars—from his father's estate.

Yet by that time, God had touched his heart and called him to service overseas. He started out in China, where he married a young Irish woman of like mind. Together, they gave away their entire portion of the Studd fortune to such ministries as George Müller's orphanage, D. L. Moody's Bible school in Chicago, the China Inland Mission, and the Salvation Army. From that point on, they trusted God to supply their needs.

Ten years of work in China were followed by six years in India, where Studd's father had become rich. C. T.'s health was not the greatest by then, and neither was his wife's. After India, he pressed on for another twenty-one years in the heart of Africa until he died and was buried there at age seventy. His passion was to share the gospel with those who had never heard of Christ. And it's the gospel passion that oozes from his nine-stanza poem, "Only One Life." Here are a couple of verses as examples.

Two little lines I heard one day,

Traveling along life's busy way;

Bringing conviction to my heart,

And from my mind would not depart;

Only one life, 'twill soon be past,

Only what's done for Christ will last.

Give me, Father, a purpose deep

In joy or sorrow Thy Word to keep;

Faithful and true whate'er the strife,

Pleasing Thee in my daily life;

Only one life, 'twill soon be past,

Only what's done for Christ will last.[8]

C. T. Studd was a man who did not let family money distract him from what was truly important in life. History tells us that his children caught his values system. Three of his daughters married Christian leaders. Some two thousand Congolese showed up for his funeral in July 1931.

I will never be the speaker and writer he was, but I am just as committed to the goals he exemplified. Of the various scriptures under the Plexiglas on my desk, this is perhaps the most compelling in my heart and mind: "This and this only has been my appointed work: getting this news to those who have never heard of God, and explaining how it works by simple faith and plain truth" (1 Timothy 2:7–8 MSG).

I hope they put that verse on my tombstone. Through the efforts of the company God has allowed us to build, I want as many people as possible to come to know Christ as Savior. Fortunately, if God blesses the values and financial arrangements that I've described in this book, then there is no reason my work will not go on long after I'm gone.

I can think of nothing that would make me happier.

When we're young, sometimes we think there's a magic key in life that will answer all the questions or solve all the problems. It's easy to think that life possesses some big secret and that when we find success, somehow we'll attain this key to unlock all the mysteries of life. But now, as part of the emeritus faculty of life, I can say that it's much simpler than that: be faithful with what God puts in front of you, and invest in the things of heaven.

Much of what I've said is summed up in the book of Matthew. Eugene Peterson, the pastor who wrote the Bible paraphrase *The Message*, puts it like this: "Don't hoard treasure down here where it gets eaten by moths and corroded by rust or—worse!—stolen by burglars. Stockpile treasure in heaven, where it's safe from moth and rust and burglars. It's obvious, isn't it? The place where your treasure is, is the place you will most want to be, and end up being" (Matthew 6:19–21).

How do you stockpile treasure in heaven?

First, stockpiling treasure is a heart issue. If I value the things of this world and what those things do for me in the here and now, then my heart's allegiance and love are plain to see.

But if the unseen things of this world hold a deeper value— things like love, grace, service, humility, and faith—then it reveals the size of my soul. I want to be remembered more for the size of my soul than for the size of my bank account. I want my children and grandchildren to identify themselves by the depth of their faith in Jesus Christ, the expanse of their love, and the richness of their grace. I want their souls to be big for the work of God's kingdom.

> I want to be remembered more for the size of my soul than for the size of my bank account.

The second thing needed to stockpile treasure is a heavenly perspective. That means doing my best to look at the world the way God sees it. This is hard, especially in our very loud digital world. It's difficult to cut through the noise and really see the world with eternal eyes. I have a heavenly perspective when I stop viewing relationships and everyday living as transactions that must happen. Our every day should be an expression of worship toward the Creator.

This perspective doesn't just show up at our door. We must cultivate it, care for it. This is not a hermit lifestyle I'm talking about. Rather, it's an engaged lifestyle in which you and I work hard at our jobs and marriages and families to glorify our Creator.

When we live with our hearts bent in, listening to God, and if we live with a heavenly perspective, then we'll grab hold of eternal things. Things that will never fade. That's what I want my resources, time, and money to work toward: building things that last forever. Hobby Lobby stores may one day shut down. Dream houses and investment portfolios will be sold, and 401(k) plans will run out. But heavenly treasure will last forever. Only when we live with an eye on eternity will we find true fulfillment. We will discover a life of joy, peace, security, hope, and meaning—a life that money can't buy. A life invested in eternity.

Notes

1. David Green, with Bill High, *Giving It All Away . . . and Getting It All Back Again: The Way of Living Generously* (Grand Rapids: Zondervan, 2017).

2. Steve and Jackie Green, *This Dangerous Book: How the Bible Has Shaped Our World and Why It Still Matters Today* (Grand Rapids: Zondervan, 2017).

3. Randy Alcorn, *The Treasure Principle* (Sisters, OR: Multnomah, 2001), 13–15.

4. See their logo at www.onehope.net.

5. William F. High, "Short-Term Recession or the Long Winter? Rethinking the Theology of Money," *Christian Research Journal* 33, no. 1 (2010): 7.

6. The following language is in the Green Stewardship Trust
   that deals with compensation of family members who work
   for the company:

   The Settlors believe that any such Green Family Member
   or spouse should be adequately and fairly compensated,
   but that compensation should not exceed what is fair and
   reasonable. Therefore, the Trustees shall cause each of the
   Green Family Companies to adopt policies and procedures
   that provide that any Green Family Member or spouse
   of a Green Family Member who is an employee or other
   service provider to any Green Family Company shall receive
   compensation and benefits which are fair and reasonable,
   but which do not exceed one and one-half times (1.5x)
   the amount of compensation and benefits which persons
   performing comparable services at the Green Family
   Companies would be entitled to receive and if there are no
   comparable positions at the Green Family Companies, then
   not to exceed one and one-half times (1.5x) the amount
   of compensation and benefits which those persons would
   otherwise be entitled to receive if they performed comparable

services with other companies of comparable size anywhere in the United States.

7. Chip Ingram, *The Genius of Generosity: Lessons from a Secret Pact Between Two Friends* (Madison, MS: Generous Church, 2011), 24.

8. Janet and Geoff Benge, *C. T. Studd: No Retreat* (YWAM, 2005).

About the Author

DAVID GREEN is the founder and CEO of Hobby Lobby, the largest privately owned arts and crafts retailer in the world. Hobby Lobby employs over 33,000 people, operates 800 stores in forty-seven states, and grosses more than $5 billion a year. Currently David serves on the Board of Reference for Oral Roberts University in Tulsa, Oklahoma. In 2013, he was honored by receiving the World Changer award and is also a past Ernst & Young national retail/consumer Entrepreneur of the Year Award recipient. In 2017, the Green family opened the Museum of the Bible in Washington, DC.

JESSAMINE COUNTY
PUBLIC LIBRARY

(859) 885-3523

Customer ID: ***1020

Items that you checked out

Title:
A generous life : 10 steps to living a life
money can't buy
ID: 32530608955249
Due: **Wednesday, February 05, 2020**

Title:
Something needs to change : a call to
make your life count in a world of urgent
need
ID: 32530609903156
Due: **Wednesday, February 05, 2020**

Total items: 2
Account balance: $0.00
1/15/2020 10:30 AM
Checked out: 3
Ready for pickup: 0

My Family
Legacy Plan

_____

_____

_____

_____

_____

_____

_____

_____

_____

_____

_____

_____
_____
_____
_____
_____
_____
_____
_____
_____
_____
_____
_____
_____
_____
_____
_____
_____